MY EXODUS

MY JOURNEY TO FREEDOM

Liza Thomas Jackson Allen

Pearly Gates Publishing, LLC, Houston, Texas (USA)

My Exodus: My Journey to Freedom

My Exodus:
My Journey to Freedom

Copyright © 2020
Liza Thomas Jackson-Allen

All Rights Reserved.
No portion of this publication may be reproduced, stored in an electronic system, or transmitted in any form or by any means (electronic, mechanical, photocopy, recording, or otherwise) without written permission from the author or publisher. Brief quotations may be used in literary reviews.

Print ISBN 13: 978-1-948853-14-9
Digital ISBN 13: 978-1-948853-15-6
Library of Congress Control Number: 2020920820

Scripture references marked AMP (Amplified Bible), KJV (King James Version), NIV (New International Version), and NKJV (New King James Version) are used with permission via Zondervan at Biblegateway.com. Public Domain.

For information and bulk ordering, contact:
Pearly Gates Publishing, LLC
Angela Edwards, CEO
P.O. Box 62287
Houston, TX 77205
BestSeller@PearlyGatesPublishing.com

DEDICATION

In loving memory of
Doris Thomas,
who will always be in my heart,
and the many others who have passed along
the way.

ACKNOWLEDGMENTS

First and foremost, I give all honor and praise to my Lord and Savior Jesus Christ, for keeping me through it all.

A special thanks to my children and grandchildren: Christopher Jackson, Jr. (CJ), "Sa'Monica," Zacorey Jackson (Corey), "Kianna," Shircrislon Jackson (Tiara), Javioun Thomas (Jav), Hillary, E'Mari, A'Mari, Cameron, Jayden, and the host of nieces, nephews, aunts, uncles, cousins, and friends.

Thank you to Shirley Thomas, Doris Thomas (Vet), Shonte Washington (Te'Layia), Eddie Thomas, Sr., Hillard Thomas, Eddie Thomas, Jr., Darleen Williams, Doris Workmon, Tina Workmon, Tyree Workmon, Jr., and Family.

To the Somerville Church of God, Immanuel Christian Fellowship, Dabney Hill Missionary Baptist Church, Texas MHMR, TRIO Support Services, Academic Advisors, Academic Coaches, Kelly Stuckey, Dr. Ren, and my Professors: Your support will never be forgotten. Thank you.

To my Prayer Partners — Marilyn Jackson, Shayne Smith, Renita Smith, Teresa Roberts, Mary Mahon, Charity Walton, and a host of others: Thank you for your encouragement.

My Exodus: My Journey to Freedom

KEY BIBLICAL PASSAGE: PSALM 34 (AMP)

The Lord, a Provider, and the One Who Rescues Me.

"I will bless the Lord at all times; His praise shall continually be in my mouth. My soul makes its boast in the Lord; the humble and downtrodden will hear it and rejoice. O magnify the Lord with me, and let us lift up His name together. I sought the Lord [on the authority of His Word], and He answered me and delivered me from all my fears. They looked to Him and were radiant; their faces will never blush in shame or confusion. This poor man cried, and the Lord heard him and saved him from all his troubles. The angel of the Lord encamps around those who fear Him [with awe-inspired reverence and worship Him with obedience], and He rescues [each of] them. O taste and see that the Lord [our God] is good; how blessed [fortunate, prosperous, and favored by God] is the man who takes refuge in Him. O [reverently] fear the Lord, you His saints (believers, holy ones); for to those who fear Him, there is no want. The young lions lack [food] and grow hungry, but they who seek the Lord will not lack any good thing. Come, you children, listen to me; I will teach you to fear the Lord [with awe-inspired reverence and worship Him with obedience]. Who is the man who desires life and loves many days, that he may see good? Keep your tongue from evil and your lips from speaking deceit. Turn away from evil and do good; seek peace and pursue it. The eyes of the Lord are toward the righteous [those with moral courage and spiritual integrity] and His ears are open to their cry. The face of the Lord is against those who do evil, to cut off the memory of them from the earth. When the righteous cry [for help], the Lord hears and rescues them from all their distress and troubles. The Lord is near to the heartbroken, and He saves those who are crushed in spirit (contrite in heart, truly sorry for their sin). Many hardships and perplexing circumstances confront the righteous, but the Lord rescues him from them all. He keeps all his bones; not one of them is broken. Evil will cause the death of the wicked, and those who hate the righteous will be *held guilty and will be condemned. The Lord redeems the soul of His servants, and none of those who take refuge in Him will be condemned."*

INTRODUCTION

In a world of "normal" people, I found myself suffering from what some people called "crazy"—a harsher term for "mental illness."

- I heard voices that were not there.
- I saw images no one else could see.
- I was happy one moment, then sad and angry at the same time.
- I awoke drenched in sweat, scared of everyone and everything around me.
- And the list goes on and on.

No one could see my pain. No one could hear my pain. No one could begin to imagine the demon that dwelt within me.

I wondered, "What do people see when they look at me?"

At that time in my life, I did not know how to relate to the world. Neither did the world know how to concur. So, I just searched my way through. My mind was floating through this dark tunnel, thinking, "Will I ever see the light? When will this darkness end…or will it ever?"

If that has ever been you—even in the slightest way—let me assure you of this one thing: Help is on the way!

One day, you will learn you are here for a reason. You may not know the reason yet, but with God's help, you will get closer to your purpose each day of your life. The Bible tells us all what we are on this earth to do:

"Let your light so shine before men, that they may see your good works and glorify your Father in Heaven"
(Matthew 5:16, NKJV).

So, you see? That is our purpose! Begin by embracing that truth and allow God to direct your path.

The Lord has always been drawing me near, even when I was running to the enemy of mental illness.

"The Lord has appeared of old to me, saying, 'Yes, I have loved you with an everlasting love; therefore, with lovingkindness, I have drawn you'"
(Jeremiah 31:3, NKJV).

My Exodus: My Journey to Freedom

TABLE OF CONTENTS

Dedication	vi
Acknowledgments	vii
Key Biblical Passage: Psalm 34 (AMP)	viii
Introduction	x
The Family	1
Life Happening	7
The Enemy's Lies	15
Betrayed	20
Ordeal	24
Over the Edge	31
Misunderstood	37
Transition	42
Struck Down	49
Learning Process	53
Tribulations	55
Mourning	63
New Beginnings	68
Hardships	75
Releasing	81
Blessings and More Blessings	84
Joy, Yet Pain	89
My Exodus	96
Closing Prayer	99

My Exodus: My Journey to Freedom

THE
FAMILY

My Exodus: My Journey to Freedom

For many years, my siblings and I grew up in a single-parent household. As the oldest of four, I knew I was different. I could never relate to those around me because of that difference.

I knew my mother loved and sacrificed a lot for me, yet even she could not understand me. Our mother-daughter relationship was just as it should have been. I knew if I needed her, she would come.

When I was younger, I did not relate to children my age. I did not have many friends in school and was far from being accepted into the "in-crowd." I wanted to go unnoticed and be left alone anyway, so acceptance was a non-factor at the time. I despised being around others and felt completely out of place.

My idea of fun was going to church, listening to God's Word. As far back as I can remember, I always wanted to know more and more about God. I believed if I learned more of His Word, it would take away the pain of being "different."

I also recall the older people sitting and talking on the porch while we children were made to play outside under the tree. At the time, there were six children in the home because my aunt and her two joined us. Since I was the oldest, I always made my siblings and cousins play the game I wanted, such as school or church. After some time, I would then distance myself from the group. Cooking was another thing I enjoyed learning and doing. To this day, I have yet to master that task.

When I was occupied with playing, cooking, or attending church, I was hopeful the voices in my head would remain at bay. I was wrong. They still tormented me.

For just a moment, imagine being a child and hearing strange voices that no one else could hear, all while not knowing from where they are coming.

I recall walking to church alone—something I did for as long as I can remember. At the time, we lived in a big white house that was three houses away from the church. I loved everyone there. The congregants took me in and cared for me while there since neither of my parents attended at the time.

My family would have big parties that often started sometime on Thursday night and didn't end until Sunday evening. The family was so big, they parked everywhere, leaving very little (if any) room for others to park.

One particular memory I have is when the church had a Homecoming service. It was when all the members—past and present—would come together in October. When they arrived, they had nowhere to park because the party at our home was ongoing.

The people from the church may not remember that occasion. My family may not recall the parties. As for me, I remember…because of the hurt.

I heard a man in church saying, "It's sad those people have no respect for the church, with their loud music, horse riding, loud talking, and profanity. Not one of them comes into the house of the Lord." Although those words hurt my spirit at the time, I now know the man meant no harm. As a matter of fact, he did not know I was one of "those people" about whom he spoke. After all, my family minded their own business. They never bothered anyone directly.

At the time, I thought I was cursed because of the life my family lived. I heard voices because of them. I saw demons because of them. I agreed with that man…to a degree. Yes, they should have turned down the music, stopped the constant horse riding while the church was in service, and shared the parking with the Home-comers. My family could have at least shown respect for the house of the Lord, even though they weren't in attendance.

Now that I am older, I want my family to come together. My family is important to me. Sadly, the only time we see each other is at a funeral. Gone are the days of the house parties, BBQing, and sitting under the trees. Everyone seems to be older and sickly now. We have lost touch with one another, especially those who have moved out of the state.

When growing up, we often visited our aunts and uncles when school wasn't in session. If we weren't with our daddy in Hearne, we would be at our other relatives' houses, spending time with their children in either Somerville or Hearne.

Uncle Boa was the best! He would come to pick all of us up, leaving no one behind. There were many good days and some dark ones spent with his family before they relocated to South Carolina.

One dark memory that sometimes floods my thoughts is when my cousin, Johnnie—who was only eight days older than I—drowned in the Little Brazos river at the age of fourteen. He has just returned home after visiting us in Snook. The month was July, and we had just turned 14 years old two months earlier.

When Johnnie passed away, the voices tormented me to no end. I walked around thinking to myself, "I'm going to die soon, too." At that point in my life, death was associated with the passing of the elderly only. When Johnnie passed, it was then I realized children die, too.

Although it may be unbelievable to some, the first time my bed literally shook out of control all night was after someone died. I laid in my bed in tears, not believing it was happening…but it did.

Relatives who passed away often came and spoke with me, but Johnnie never did. I didn't understand why.

My Uncle Pony was one who talked to me. He would take me to the road each night. No matter how hot or cold it was, he would take me to the road. When the voices came and tormented me, it was the road that would calm me down. I'm sure Pony understood the importance of me going to the road. When I was three years old, Pony passed away. He may have died in the natural, but he is still with me and very much alive in my heart.

One day, Pony told me Uncle Paul and Uncle Tyree would take on his job, and they would be there to protect me from danger. Both did an excellent job, if I must say. He was blind in the natural, but his supernatural eyes were opened wide. Uncle Paul was a prayer warrior. Our room was next to his, and we would hear him praying for hours at a time. During his prayer time, he would call out our names one by one. Whether drunk or sober, he prayed the fervent prayer over all of our lives, as described in James 5:16. In those prayers, he was canceling the devil's assignment over our lives.

I'm comforted in knowing he wasn't the only person praying for me.

Living in the darkness of mental illness made my life a living hell. I cursed people out and called them every name but a child of the Living God. Because I was hurting, I wanted others to hurt as well, yet no one could come close to feeling my pain.

LIFE HAPPENING

Everyone who knows me, either from working with or just being around me, knows I had a real and an imaginary life. My family and friend would often laugh at and make fun of me. They thought I was playing when I said certain things that were real-life situations. Some of my cousins started to call me "Real Life." I know they took me as a joke, but that was okay. It hid the pain of who I truly was on the inside. The Bible verse, James 1:8, was me all the way:

"He is a double-minded man, unstable in all his ways" (NKJV).

I was double-minded and unstable, which led me down a path to destruction.

*"There is a way that seems right to a man,
but its end is the way of death"*
(Proverbs 16:25, NKJV).

When I say to you the way of destruction ends in death, I mean every word.

At the age of 19, I started dating and living the life I thought I should live. No longer did I listen to the voice of God. The path of destruction was set before me. Those dark voices were louder, and I listened to them constantly. Two failed marriages later, all hope seemed lost. The voices prohibited me from having healthy, full, and loving relationships.

My first husband was a loving man. I did not know how to treat him, as he was my first real relationship. I gave him my all—my innocence, my peace, my love, my joy…and my demons of mental illness. He received from me every insecurity

I had, every voice with influence, every panic attack, every moment of depression and mania, every emotion, and all the side effects I had from the illness—all in one package. Truth be told, I'm surprised he stayed as long as he did.

When I started having children, my paranoia was the worst. The voices would tell me I was ugly, no one wanted me, and that my husband would leave me. When the voices told me I could not have children (even though I was pregnant), I believed the lies. People used to say things like, "For someone who's pregnant, I can't tell." The voices fed on their comments, leading me to believe their lies all the more.

At 32 weeks, I went into labor with my oldest son and gave birth to him at 34 weeks. We nicknamed him CJ. During that time, the voices really tore me down. They would say I was being punished for having a child out of wedlock and would suffer for the sins I had committed.

Shortly after his birth, my son was scheduled to be transferred to Scott N White in Temple from St. Joseph Hospital in Bryan. I remember praying and asking God for them not to take my baby. I asked God, "Please let us remain in Bryan." We didn't have much money, and because our son wasn't due until December, travel to Temple simply wasn't in our budget.

Well, God worked it out! My son and I stayed at St. Joseph!

In October 1994, it rained and rained. The event became known as "The October Overflow." I recall the Brazos River rising higher than it has ever done in years. I didn't get to see it, though, because I was still in the hospital recovering from giving birth.

When a woman has a baby, the expectation is that the child will go home with her when released. I didn't have my son with me because he had to remain under the hospital's care. I went home and was tormented with delusions, panic attacks, mania, and depression. However, I didn't let any of those things stop me from visiting my baby daily. I would arrive at the start of visiting hours and wouldn't leave until visiting hours ended.

Three days after my release, I had what I call a "setback." Because I had been moving around too much, I started bleeding and cramping. My body was hurting as if I were preparing to give birth all over again. I suffered horribly, all while not having the relationship with God like I had in the past.

Still, I was grateful that the Lord allowed my baby to remain at St. Joseph in the Neonatal Unit. I'm also blessed to say that during that time, God started to heal me.

My son was born weighing 4 lbs., 11 oz. God blessed his father and me to bring him home, weighing only five ounces less. That was God's favor!

> *"And Jesus increased in wisdom and stature,*
> *and in favor with God and men"*
> (Luke 2:52, NKJV).

I did not know that passage of scripture at the time, but knowing it now, it will be forever etched in my heart. It has brought me through many challenging situations.

Although God healed my body, my mental illness remained untreated and got worse. Despite what I was going through, my son's father chose to hang in there with me.

Having an ill child and working a very stressful job only proved to pile on the pain. I loved my job, but it was challenging. It wasn't the people I worked with directly that made it that way; it was the other staff members. They would show favoritism to some and not others. Some, I consider to be close friends still. I may not see or talk to them often, but I consider them my friends.

I worked very hard, even though I had to contend with my "issues." I loved the people I worked with so much, I missed out on my son's first Christmas, taking his first step, and saying his first word. I went to work sick—tired from working long hours due to being understaffed and working alongside those who lacked on-the-job training due to the lack of staff.

Then, one day, something happened that really triggered my illness. When my son was nine months old, he got sick. His father picked me up from work around midnight. When I got home, I took a bath and headed straight for bed with my son in my arms. All I wanted to do was go to sleep.

Just as I always did, I held my son in my arms as I slept. I had a habit of putting his face to mine or putting a finger under his nose to make sure he was still breathing. After doing so, I awoke in a panic. I didn't feel him breathing!

That happened on a Sunday morning. I had just taken my son to the doctor that previous Friday, and he was diagnosed with an upper respiratory infection. That Sunday, he was still feverish. When I called the job to tell them I wouldn't be in due to my son being sick, they said that due to many employees out of work already due to allegations lodged against them, they really needed me to come to work.

I remember having to leave early one day when we did not have enough coverage, and a patient got into a supply closet after I left, getting some type of chemical in his eyes. I was so hurt by that because I made sure all my individuals were bathed and put to bed before leaving. I had asked for someone to cover me before I left, but the shift coordinator said it would be okay to leave because we didn't have the additional coverage available.

So, there I was with my lifeless child in my arms. I know it was God who gave me the strength to scream for my son's father. We jumped into our car in our pajamas and rushed our lifeless baby to Humana Hospital. When we arrived, the medical team ran him to the back. I was crying hysterically. The nurses were so mean to us, asking questions like, "How did you let him get so bad off?" A nurse told us they had to put the IV in his tiny foot because they could not place it in his temple, saying he was too dehydrated. Shortly after, a doctor came out and told us it was not looking good for our son.

BUT GOD!

The staff treated my son's father and me like we had the plague! When we asked them questions, we received short answers in response. No one knew the voices in my head were back to the task of tormenting me to no end while my child fought for his life.

Around 9:00 a.m., an investigator from my job came to the hospital, asking questions about the incident with the man getting into the supply closet. I told him, "I take full responsibility." I had received many awards at my job for going above and beyond. While still on probation when that incident happened, I was given a verbal reprimand instead of being fired. That was nothing but God's grace and mercy seeing me through.

After the investigator left, like clockwork, Child Protective Services came to ask my son's father and me questions, to include, "How did your child get into this condition?" I was able to show her where I had taken him to the doctor on Friday and his respiratory infection diagnosis. I also mentioned he was born prematurely and that I had difficulties with his birth.

"Do not be afraid. Stand still, and see the salvation of the Lord, which He will accomplish for you today. The Lord will fight for you, and you shall hold your peace. When the enemy comes in like a flood, the Spirit of the Lord will lift up a standard against him"
(Exodus 14:12-14, NKJV).

I wasn't living a saved lifestyle. I lived with my son's father, and we weren't married at the time. All my life, I've heard voices. Once I left the church, the voices brought on every attack of the devil. He had free reign to come at me from all directions.

The voices told me everyone was trying to take my son from me, including his father. They said his father was totally against me and that I have no one to turn to.

My son's father was very outgoing. He loved being around people, which is the total opposite of me. I would talk and be cordial, but my comfort zone was being alone or around very few family members.

For two days, my son's condition did not improve. I'm grateful for the small circle of family and friends who stood beside me as I dealt with that crisis. When everyone else had to leave, I remained with my son as he fought for his life in the Neonatal Unit.

On the third day, as we stood looking in at him, we noticed he was kicking the tent off him in the incubator. The doctor approached us and said, "He is a fighter! We're going to remove the oxygen tent and move him to a room. I remember him coming in lifeless and not seeing any improvement. Now, he is doing the most!"

After being moved to a room, he still had to receive oxygen treatments. When the nurses came to administer them, my son would fight with them. While my son fought the nurses, I fought the demons on the inside of me.

THE ENEMY'S LIES

The voices told me I was not a good parent and that no one loved me. The only person who made me feel complete was my son, and he was trying to leave me. I felt worthless. No one wanted to be around me.

I would sometimes wake my son's father in the middle of the night when I had a panic attack. He would say to me, "I don't know who you are today. Are we going to have a good day or a bad one?" The attacks grew progressively worse as the voices grew progressively louder and attacked me every moment of the day. The voices taunted, "You worship that job so much, you almost lost your baby!"

The doctor prescribed a medication to help me, but my son's father threw them away. He blamed the medicine for my mood swings that were coming so fast and often, I was losing control at home. I needed to go back to work to try and hold things together while blocking the commotion from the voices as they tormented me. I put in for the 6:00 a.m. to 2:00 p.m. shift, for which I was approved. However, the shift often had me getting off at 10:00 p.m. or whenever I was relieved. My job kept me so busy, I had no time to focus on the voices playing with my head.

I was also working so hard, I failed to notice some of the signs my body gave me. One day, our car had a flat tire. While my son's father was fixing the flat, the vehicle somehow fell and knocked me down. I felt so sick afterward, so my son's father took me to the doctor.

Wouldn't you know? I was pregnant again.

I should have known. I should have paid attention to the signs. When I was pregnant, the mood swings would become more severe…and the voices would act up even more.

They would tell me my coworkers were talking about me "always being pregnant," even though I hadn't revealed to anyone on the job that I was again with child. I wanted my pregnancy to remain a secret.

The voices — as bad as they were — and the fatigue of working while pregnant started to take its toll on me.

When I got off work one day, my son's father had a house full of my family. This particular day, a cousin was smoking in the house. "My child has RSV!" I screamed, then asked everyone to leave.

Well, things got out of hand, and a fight broke out between three other pregnant ladies and me. Everyone knew the other three were pregnant, but no one knew about my pregnancy. After the scuffle, my son's father and I left, fearing someone would call the authorities. Before leaving, though, someone mentioned calling the police, to which my son's father replied, "They're all going to jail! Nie's pregnant, too!" (I was four months pregnant at the time.) Now, everyone knew. The cat was out of the bag.

After the "big reveal," the voices and hallucinations were so bad, I couldn't distinguish between what was real and what was not. I couldn't talk to my son's father because he didn't understand me.

While at work one day, an individual attacked me and made me fall. I landed on my tailbone, which sent a shockwave up my body. I had to go to the doctor because the fall caused me to bleed badly. With the problems I had with my previous pregnancy, I was very concerned about carrying this baby to term.

On the way to the doctor's office, the questions came back-to-back:

"Would the doctor have to take my baby?"

"Would I lose my baby to a miscarriage?"

In an effort to have me carry to term, the doctor immediately placed me on complete bed rest.

Depression took up residence in my mind, and I started seeing dark images again. While lying in bed or on the sofa, dark spirits would come to visit me—and I was wide awake! I could feel them trying to pull me through the bed or sofa. I wasn't able to cry out for help. All I could do was lie there, fighting and waiting until they passed over.

Being confined to bed felt like a death sentence. I was mean to everyone who came around. I felt worthless. The only person I wanted near me was my son. He was my peace. He needed me, and I needed him to calm the illness that dwelt inside of me.

Months later, I gave birth to a healthy 6 lb., 6 oz. baby boy we named Zaconey after I had a severe panic attack and went into labor. My mother and Tyree were the ones who drove me to Brazos Valley Medical Center that day.

Each pregnancy affected the illness within me in one way or another. My mind was triggered by certain people, too. I would look at them and go into a mad rage for whatever the reason. Certain foods would unleash the tormenting spirit, and specific noises would trigger the voices to mock me at every turn.

Those things really happened to me, yet no one seemed to understand or try to help me.

BETRAYED

I learned about my last pregnancy while at work. The same woman who attacked me on the job previously struck again. She kicked me in the stomach and knocked me down.

Immediately, I felt unusual and started having bad hallucinations. They were awful and scary. I went to the doctor and found out I was pregnant…again. Oh, my goodness!

At the time, my son's father hung out with my brothers quite often. The voices found it their business to tell me he was cheating on me. Sadly, they were correct this time.

It was a Friday night. My sons' father and my brothers went out for a night on the town. I wasn't going anywhere. I was so far along in my pregnancy, I couldn't even button my clothes anymore. That night, however, the voices convinced me to go to Bryan. I asked my mother to watch our sons while I went out. Once in Bryan, I saw our car parked at a store. I quickly approached and saw one of my brothers driving, with the other in the passenger's seat. When I opened the door, I saw my son's father and a girl sitting in the backseat with a jacket over them. I couldn't believe it! I reached in and grabbed him. At the same time, my brother grabbed me and carried me away to my car, all while talking to me to try and calm me down. A moment later, my son's father drives up and tells my brother to get in. I tried to get them to stop, but they wouldn't!

The voices took complete control. I vaguely remember chasing them down in the car. I remember bits and pieces of the moments that followed, including me driving badly. I do know things did not turn out well for my ex and me. Our relationship was no longer the same after that night.

Weeks later, I gave birth to our daughter. Our family unit was no more. My son's father moved on with his life, and eventually, I moved on with mine.

During that transition, my family was my strength. Whenever I felt myself losing control, I would drop off my children at my mother's house.

If you have ever suffered from any form of mental illness, you can relate when I say that you do not want to feel what you experience. Recovery is not as easy as merely bouncing out of the mood you are in. There were many days I told myself, "Snap out of it! You are bigger than this!" I cried often and wanted life to end. I was tired of suffering and being pulled in different directions.

When my ex left, our children suffered the most. He often promised he would come and never show up. I blamed myself for the hurt my children endured. After all, he left because of me. The voices took every opportunity they had to remind me of that fact. Nonetheless, I had to work diligently to protect my children from anyone hurting them in any way, shape, or form.

After being deceived by my ex, there was no trust in him whatsoever. Being honest here, when he didn't pick up our children, I was glad. I felt I needed to protect them from his deceit. He had a court order for visitation, and he had his parental rights. Thankfully, he does not push the issue to get them when scheduled. My children are my life.

Those times when our children were with my family, I always knew they were safe. That was all that mattered to me. I can't say the same when they were with him, and that concerned me.

As a result of our family's break up, the voices had a field day with me.

"You're worthless!"

"You don't deserve those children!"

"You are nothing!"

"You are a nobody!"

I now know they were all the words spoken by the father of lies: Satan.

GOD tells me that I am *"fearfully and wonderfully made; marvelous are thy works; and that my soul knoweth right well"* (Psalm 139:14, KJV).

For those who know me, they will tell you I will praise the Lord, no matter who's around. It was He who took me—someone who thought she was useless and nothing—and made me whole. Only God can truly transform someone from the inside!

ORDEAL

On August 19, 2002, my baby girl Tiara started pre-k. She was so excited about her new chapter as she left me to go to school.

At home and all alone, I found myself constantly worrying about something happening to my children when they were out of my sight.

Well…

On Friday, August 23, 2002, I received a call from my daughter's school telling me she fell off the monkey bars. My mother and sister picked her up from school and drove her to the hospital. I agreed to meet them there, and we arrived at the same time.

I noticed the red scarf she had tied around her neck that held her arm tightly in place. Knowing how dramatic I could be, my daughter said, "Mama, stop crying! My arm isn't broken, and my neck isn't either." She hugged me tightly to stop me from going into hysterics.

The Emergency Room physician put her arm into a sling and told me I would have to take her to see a specialist. We take her to the doctors closer to home, and they immediately began working on her arm. They set it back in place then set it in a cast.

Before that incident, my ex and I discussed reconciling our differences. I thought I needed him because I felt as if I were failing our children. The voices told me I wasn't protecting them from getting hurt and that I needed my ex with us at all times. Perhaps the voices were correct. My daughter had a broken arm, after all.

When my ex brought pain medication for our daughter, he told me he was coming home for good. (At the time, he was going back and forth from house to house. He would stay with his girlfriend for a while and then come back to me — something he did for years.) Tiara broke her arm on Friday, but my ex did not come until Sunday.

August 25, 2002, changed my life forever. My ex came to the house around 4:00 p.m. that afternoon. However, he did not come alone. He brought his girlfriend along. I asked them to leave, and they refused.

His girlfriend's children were with me at the time, as they sometimes spent the weekend with my children and me. When my ex and his girlfriend would go out, I would watch the children, but she never came to my house for a visit.

I know what you're thinking, and it's okay. We lived that way because I had low self-esteem, thinking no one else wanted me and that he was the only one who found value in me.

(Thank You, Lord, for deliverance! I know my worth now!)

As I stated, they would not leave, which caused a serious argument. She even had the audacity to say to me, "We're not going anywhere!"

The voices in my head spoke up. "She already has your husband. The courts make you send your children to their house. Now, she is here trying to take over your home. All you have left is your home!"

I continued asking them to leave. They kept refusing.

The voices were really going in on me. Then, we all got into a fight. She ended up in the emergency room.

I ended up in jail, charged with Aggravated Assault with Bodily Injury and Criminal Mischief. How was that right?! They were the ones who came to my home and violated my space! My daughter was hurt. I was minding my own business. I didn't strike out first, yet I was the one who ended up in jail in my red pajamas shorts and a white t-shirt with no bra.

When the police came, they would not take me to jail. They told my family someone else would have to bring me. I recall there being a yard full of people from the neighborhood. I also remember being out of control. After my family talked me into turning myself in, my sister was the one who took me to turn myself in to the authorities.

I remember one officer saying to me, "You are not so bad without your crowd!" What he did not know was that I was worse on the inside. The voices told me that everyone was against me. I wanted them to kill me.

I was especially upset about the officer telling me my home was community property, even though my ex and I never resided in the house together. What made it community property in the state of Texas was that he and I were still married. As such, he could bring whomever he wanted to MY home.

Although all three of us were fighting, the police arrested only me. My ex and his girlfriend were allowed to go free.

The voices were tearing me up. I was put in a cell with other women, some of which I knew. That "arrangement" didn't last long, though. The sweet and innocent woman the ladies knew began to show them the demons that tormented me. With swiftness, an officer moved me to a different cell where I was all alone.

When I asked to go to the restroom, I was told, "This isn't the Hilton. Use the toilet in your cell." There was no way I was going to use that nasty toilet, so I went on myself. At the time, it seemed like a good idea. Later, I saw I made a big mistake. I was still wearing my pajamas and had yet to be given the orange jumpsuit I expected. Instead, I received a wool blanket. Wool and urine do not go well together. Plus, I have sensitive skin.

All night long, I fought with the demons inside of me. Eventually, I drifted off to sleep. My mother called to see if I was okay. "She's fine. She's not going anywhere," the officer said. There was no way the demons were going to let me off that easily.

The voices talked all night. I even talked back to them for a while, got mad at them, and tried to reason with them. I told the demons I missed my children. In response, they said, "Your children are fine. They're better off without you."

I was sure my ex would hurt my children just to hurt me worse than he had already. I began talking to God, asking Him to please not let anyone take my children away. A distinct voice said to me, "No one can take them. You can give them away."

I was released from jail Monday, August 26th. The next day, Texas Mental Health and Mental Retardation (MHMR) in Caldwell ordered me to get a mental health screening. I was diagnosed with Schizoaffective Disorder, mania, and depression. I've been a Texas MHMR patient ever since. They prescribed me medication right away, all while the voices laughed at my doctor. As the year progressed, I came to respect that man.

With every caseworker they switched out, I fell deeper and deeper into depression. I despised change and felt as if no one wanted to provide consistent care for me. It seemed like once I started to like someone, they would leave me. After some time, I refused to allow myself to get close to any other caretaker.

Once I was back home, my sister would come and check on me every day. No matter what, she made it a point to stop by. She made sure I ate and took my medicine while there.

One Saturday night, we went out, and my sister met someone. They started to date, but her concern remained with me. She did not want me to be alone, so her friend introduced me to his friend.

Ladies, please hear me: Let GOD lead you. Please do not settle for "the hook-up"!!! My hook-up became my second ex-husband.

My sister and I would often go on double-dates. The "friend" and I spent a lot of time alone, too. We would go for walks, go fishing (something we both loved to do), and he liked to stay at home—just like I did.

A year before I met him, I had a conversation with my sister and grannie. I told them, "I am getting married!"

"Oh, wow! Who is the lucky fellow?" they asked.

"I don't know, but in three years on my birthday, I'm going to be married."

My sister and grannie laughed and said, "Okay!"

Three days after moving in with me, my second ex-husband and I had a serious argument. He said to me, "Women would normally put on a front and not let people know who they really were until a year into the relationship!"

As for me, I had so many people living inside of me, they all showed up in those three days.

OVER THE EDGE

On November 19, 2004, it happened. I tried to end it all. After fighting my mother and sister, the voices I heard said they were talking about me. I kept hearing my sister cursing at me and, when I would confront her, she would say, "I didn't say anything to you!" She was not one to back down from a fight, so we went at it. My mother and father took up for her. In my mind, I felt threatened and tried to protect myself from them.

That day, my son had an appointment—one that caused me great distress. When I finally came to myself, I was so enraged, I didn't know what was real or what was fake. On the way to my son's appointment, I consumed three different medications: Depakote, Zoloft, and Sequel.

I took a 30-day supply of each…all at once.

I manage to make it through my son's appointment and then headed to Bryan High, where my ex worked. I went there because I wanted him to get off work and pick up our other son and take him to school for me.

At the time, my ex and I were separated and going through a divorce. We got married on February 17, 2000, and were officially divorced in July 2005.

My ex didn't take off work.

My son and I made it to my boyfriend's job. He worked for a company in Snook, which was a long drive from Bryan. Along the way, I began to feel the medicines taking effect. Zacorey was in the car with me, and I knew I had to get him to safety as I slipped in and out of consciousness. I struggled to make it there, but we made it, nonetheless. When my boyfriend asked my son what was wrong with me, of course, my son did not know.

I prayed. "Lord, if it is not my time to die, please don't let me die." Still, I was tired of the voices, anxiety, depression, and constant mood swings from happy to angry. I was tired of waking up to severe panic attacks and not being able to be helped. Dark spirits that tormented my soul would soon be no more. I no longer wanted to continue hurting my family and could not tame the barrage of emotions that we out of control. Even with the medication, nothing worked to change the course of my life. Anytime I felt stressed, I would quickly lose control. The fight with my mother and sister for no good reason whatsoever proved that. I could not continue to live that way.

My boyfriend rushed me home and put me in the shower. He then called a close friend of mine who is like a sister to me, and she came over. She then put me in her car and took me to Burleson St. Joseph Hospital, where I was in and out of consciousness. I remember having the meanest nurse ever asking me questions. I recall seeing my son looking at and calling for me. I tried reaching out to him, but I couldn't move.

"Code Blue! We are losing her!" screamed a nurse. The last thing I heard before losing all consciousness was, "We are not going to lose you today!"

When I woke up, my chest and throat were so sore, and a breathing tube was down my throat. My stomach hurt from all the charcoal the medical staff had to put in my stomach to absorb all the medication.

NOTE: If you have never overdosed, please do not do it. There are severe consequences for your actions, including countless bouts with diarrhea.

My mother, sister, Shonte, and my three children were at my bedside. I didn't want to wake up all the way. The voices taunted me:

"You couldn't even die the right way."

I remember being awakened by a police officer asking what happened, although he already knew. I tried to take my life, but God spared me. The officer told my family I would likely be sent to Austin Mental Hospital upon my release.

Once again, Texas MHMR came and did an assessment. Just as the officer predicted, they wanted to send me to Austin. Instead, my family offered to watch over me at home to ensure I was safe.

To keep me from being sent away, my family took on the responsibility of watching over me around the clock. I felt so bad. They sacrificed their time by spending time at both the hospital and then at home with me.

My children looked at me with disappointment. My suicide attempt affected my middle son the most. Today, he has a hard time dealing with hearing about anyone who has committed suicide. He says they are selfish and only thinking about themselves.

I respectfully disagree. I thought about those I hurt around me as well as myself.

In Mark 5:2-5, I believe the demonic man cuts himself to be free of the demons. He tried to release them to keep from hurting both those around him and himself.

I believe when people try to hurt themselves to keep from hurting those they love, they actually do more bad than good. I now know we should look to God for refuge and healing.

> *"I will lift up my eyes to the hills from which comes my help? My help comes from the Lord, who made Heaven and earth. He will not allow your foot to be moved; He who keeps you will not slumber"*
> (Psalm 121:1-3, NKJV).

For quite a while, my family walked on pins and needles around me. No one dared to utter a word about what I was going through. I was like a sore topic for the longest time and believed some of them thought I wanted to be that way, making it even hard to deal with.

The voices told me I was better of not being alive—and I truly believed them. Why was I the only one hearing them, though? They screamed so loudly and continuously put me down. Dark spirits were always on the wall or ceiling, and they continued shaking my bed while trying to pull me through. No one knew the depths of my daily struggle. I would get up and wait for the torment to begin. Their mission was evident: not to kill but constantly torture me.

At any given moment, I expected the day to turn into one where I had to fight because I was so tired of people making fun of me to my face. I was tired of the degradation. The same people who treated me like they loved me were the main ones out to get me—or so the voices said.

I thought everyone in the world was out to get me. It was just a matter of time.

MISUNDERSTOOD

It was easy to believe every put down the voices spoke to me, mainly because I knew no one understood me. When I was around, people felt very uncomfortable. Conversely, I felt the same being around them, so I distanced myself.

Once I was well enough to be home alone, I continued to call and check on my family. My sister told me I phoned so much, my children ran from the phone when it rang. She told me how every morning when I called to speak to my children before they went to school, they would run and hide in different rooms to keep from coming to the phone. She thought it was funny and would eventually make all three of them get on the phone to talk to me.

My mental illness made me feel as if my own children didn't want me around. I felt like an insignificant nobody. As I reflect on those days, I can understand why my children didn't want to talk to me: I would be on the phone for hours, asking them countless questions.

"How are you doing?"

"How are your grades?"

"Who are you hanging around?"

I wanted to know every little detail about their lives.

To keep them out of trouble, I encouraged them to participate in sports. I wanted them to succeed in life, where I've fallen short due to my illness. I didn't let anyone tell my children they could not excel in life. For example, although my oldest son is short, he loved playing basketball. I know he had challenges, but I never stopped encouraging him to pursue his dreams. Although I had failed at living my life to the fullest, I was never going to let my children follow my same path.

In October 2008, I started a new job and was in orientation from 8:00 a.m. to 5:00 p.m. during the week. One day, my children had a football game in Milano. Anyone who knows me knows I never miss any of my children's games. Mental illness and all, I went everywhere my children went.

That particular day, I thought their game was scheduled to start at 6:00. I had to drive from Giddings to Milano and knew nothing about how to get to my destination. I recall not having much money that day, either. After praying and talking to my sister, I managed to arrive around 6:30. Thankfully, the game hadn't started yet, as they were still warming up. I never wanted my sons to play football due to my fear of them getting hurt.

Without fail, the voices showed up and showed out. They were telling me one of my children would be hurt.

I spoke to those in the stands I knew and had a seat in a corner by myself, praying the entire time.

The game began. My sons' team, the Blue Jays, were doing well. Both of my sons were running plays, and CJ ran the ball. As I sat in the stands, I envisioned something terrible happening. As if in slow motion, my worst fear became a reality.

In my mind, the children weren't children anymore; they were giants running after my baby. All at once, the giants piled on top of him. I knew he was hurt. I jumped out of my seat and prepared to run onto the field, but two good friends grabbed me and held me tight. I prayed my baby was okay.

As he was helped off the field, I could tell my baby was hurt. Everyone always says I overreact to everything, but in this case, I knew his arm was broken. How did I know? I saw how it dangled in the most unnatural way. No one else in the stands saw it, but I did.

At first, my children didn't know I was there. That was until Zacorey looked into the stands and saw me. He then pointed me out to CJ.

For years, almost every time I closed my eyes, I would wake up drenched in sweat, remember the look on my child's face when he saw me there. It took everything in me not to run out onto that field to protect my child from "the giants."

CJ didn't want to go to the emergency room. His coach told him he likely experienced a sprain, but I knew it was broken. Of course, my son listened to his coach. After all, his coach was the smart one, and I was the crazy one. Against the coach's advisement, I took my son to the hospital, where he was diagnosed with a broken arm.

The next day, CJ had to see a specialist. Since I had just started my new job, I couldn't take off, so my mother and sisters took him to his appointment. I wanted to always be there for my children but knew I often needed my family's help and support. As I thought about their friends likely knowing I suffered from a mental illness, I thought it best that they stay with my mother and sisters. They would be safe with them.

I was mentally ill and did not understand it was a disease. I believed I was cursed, with the destination being Hell's fire. I just knew no one else in the world suffered as I did. In no way could they have experienced such pain or shame.

TRANSITION

I once believed the voices. Now, I believe my God who art in Heaven. He tells me, "Liza, you are fearfully and wonderfully made. Marvelous are My works, Liza; not yours." Alone, I know this illness is too much for me to bear.

"I can do all things through Christ who strengthens me"
(Philippians 4:13, NKJV).

Every day, I will bless the Lord and sing praises to His Name. I would not be here today were it not for God saving me.

It is a constant battle, not wanting to be around people you believe are talking about you. You walk through the mall, see someone laughing, and believe in your heart they are talking about you. You are in the movies sitting at the very front, hear laughter, and think it's about you.

There were times I confronted women in a vehicle like mine, thinking it was my husband in the car with her. Of course, some of my suspicions were triggered by events that occurred with both of my ex-husbands. They cheated on me several times.

I have learned to tame the voices with God's Word.

"'For your Maker is your husband, The Lord of Hosts is His name; and your Redeemer is the Holy One of Israel; He is called the God of the whole earth. For the Lord has called you like a woman forsaken and grieved in spirit, like a youthful wife when you were refused,' says your God"
(Isaiah 54:5-6, NKJV).

I now know how a husband is supposed to treat his wife and how a wife should treat her husband. That verse is healing to my soul.

God will never curse at me or cheat on me. God will never put me down. When I am sick, He takes very good care of me, in sickness and good health. God wants to see me prosper as my soul prospers. God builds me up.

My job is to honor God and love Him totally. I must submit everything totally to Him. I must release my independence and humble myself under Him. I can no longer believe the lies of the mental illness from which I suffered. I must admit there are struggles to acquire freedom from the mental illness that strikes against me.

Adding two unfaithful ex-husbands to the fire was very explosive. I felt like less than a woman — and the voices served to confirm that about me. Not one but two husbands rejected me. My second husband cheated on me with my ex-sister-in-law, and our relationship was rocky ever since.

As I was renewing my relationship with Christ, He was strengthening me.

On April 27, 2007, I had to have what I thought was a simple same-day surgery. The doctor told me if I did not have the surgery, I could die. I never feared death before, although I had often longed for it. That day was different, though. I was scared something was going to go wrong. I wrote letters to all my loved ones, telling them how much I loved them. The situation before me was that serious.

My then-boyfriend told me when I recovered from the surgery, he wanted me to be his wife. We would no longer live in sin. I was still uneasy. The hospital's Chaplain came and prayed with my family and me that everything would go well.

That day was also my middle son's birthday, so my family took him out to celebrate the day as I had asked of them. When they returned, I remember being in so much pain, I couldn't walk—and the voices returned, tormenting me. I felt as if I was going completely insane. I was hot, cold, happy, sad, angry, and in immense pain straight from the pits of Hell. I kept hitting the morphine button, but relief would not come.

A week later, I was released from the hospital. Once home, my boyfriend literally waited on me hand and foot. He would not let me do anything.

I had a panic attack that caused me to strip off all my clothes and to put my head in the freezer. I took cold showers until I had chills running through my body. I could hardly walk but kept going from room to room. When I attempted to go outside, I couldn't open the door because I was weak and delirious. I didn't know who I was or what was going on.

After coming back to myself, I married my second husband on May 12, 2007.

God drew me closer to Him in the process. He made right where I went wrong. I read my Bible and talked to God, telling Him all about my hurts and how I hurt others. I did not know real life from imaginary. I asked Him questions and read scriptures to suit my situation. Scripture became real to me. God's Word began to get me out of some bad situations.

As I allowed God to lead my life, I started talking to Him like I used to speak to the voices that tormented my soul. We would have many conversations about my day. I still did not feel comfortable around people, but in God's presence, I felt safe. He never has, and I know He never will hurt me.

I know my mother doesn't mean to, but she hurts me when she fails to understand the issues I have with the voices. In fact, she makes fun of them. She says things like, "They better sit down today!" Although my sisters and I are very close, they don't understand me, either. I love them, and I know they love me. I suppose that's all that matters.

My poor children have lived with my mood swings, hallucinations, the voices, headaches, and temper tantrums. They have bore witness to it all. They lived through my depression—when I stayed locked away in my room for months and would not come out. There were also times I was so high on Sequel, I couldn't even hold a real conversation. Who wants to put their children through those things? I know I didn't, but I was in a state of helplessness.

My children always helped me survive. I love them with everything in me and have always wanted the very best for them. Amid my struggles, I needed them to achieve greatness. I put them in sports. I tried to make sure they stayed on top of their grades. They had the latest "everything" their hearts desired.

As for me, I didn't need anything. Neither did I deserve anything. All I had went to them and my then-husband. I believed I was just a crazy person who only deserved misery and torment as those around me lived their lives from day to day.

"And when He had come out of the boat, immediately there met Him out of the tombs a man with an unclean spirit, who had his dwelling among the tombs, and no one could bind him, not even with chains, because he had often been bound with shackles and chains. And the chains had been pulled apart by him, and the shackles broken in pieces; neither could anyone tame him. And always, night and day, he was in the mountains and in the tombs, crying out and cutting himself with stones"
(Mark 5:2-5, KJV).

I was trapped in my own little world. My children, family, and friends were good, and that's all that mattered to me.

God then spoke to me much louder. Deuteronomy 28:1-13 describes what God has for me. He says I am the head and not the tail; I am above and not beneath. 1 John 4:4 tells me that greater is He who lives on the inside of me than he that is in the world. What I was missing is found in 1 Peter 2:910 (NKJV):

"But you are a chosen generation, a royal priesthood, a holy nation, His own special people, that you may proclaim the praises of Him who called you out of darkness into His marvelous light; who once were not a people but are now the people of God, who had not obtained mercy but now have obtained mercy."

It seemed I was messing up everything and everywhere, yet I continued living in the darkness.

STRUCK DOWN

My Exodus: My Journey to Freedom

God's Word tells me He called me out of the darkness. I will be the first to confess: I was in total darkness.

During my 9th-grade year of high school, I fell behind in Math. My teacher was concerned and called for a meeting with my mother. Together, they decided to put me in a lower Math class. I was crushed. The voices told me I would never succeed.

The way my body was built kept me from participating in sports. My breasts were a size DD by the time I reached 11th grade. I couldn't run because of my breasts. They were actually larger than most of my teachers' breasts. I was called 'Dolly Parton,' even by family members. I hated my breasts and myself. I recall a friend telling me she would "use them big girls to her advantage." As for me, I couldn't wait to get them cut off. I thought doing that would make the voices go away.

I had the surgery, and my insecurities went away. However, surgery seemed to enhance the problem I had with the voices, hallucinations, and torment.

Imagine being high on pain killers when you are not in touch with reality. I could never imagine myself addicted to drugs. My thoughts already controlled me, and I hated allowing anything whatsoever to have that power.

Living life in total darkness, I tended to do strange things. I started hanging out with people I knew were not real friends; they were users. I had a car, and they were walking, so they chose to hang with me. They had no job. I was the only one with an income. I was supposed to be their friend, but the only time they called was when they needed something. They even made fun of me in my face. I loved to dance but have no rhythm. That didn't matter because I danced to the voices' tune, which gave me the last laugh.

I thought I was having fun until one day, the voices told me, "Liza, you know they are not your friends. They make fun of you to your face, and they know you are not afraid to fight for them. Plus, you're the only one with income and a ride." After that revelation, I became bitter.

When I called my "friends" to see if the voices were correct, they never answered. My heart grew more and more bitter toward them all. I was so enraged, I wanted to go and kick in each of their doors. I wanted them to feel the pain of being rejected. I was ready to fight!

"Therefore, you have no excuse or defense or justification, O man, whoever you are who judges and condemns another. For in posing as judge and passing sentence on another, you condemn yourself, because you who judge are habitually practicing the very same things (that you censure and denounce)"
(Romans 2:1, AMP).

Wow! Talk about a wake-up call! The behavior I entertained would only serve to get me into trouble. I was unequally yoked with those people. We had nothing in common. Even though I suffered from mental illness, I did have morals and somewhat of a relationship with Christ.

My family truly loves me. If I were around their friends when I spoke, they knew something was different about me and would just laugh it off. They always had their friends treat me with dignity and respect, whereas the others I called friends would always put me down.

People must know your worth. Please do not settle for rejection. That's a spirit, and it will attach itself to you. Being unequally yoked never works out. Instead, I encourage you to find peace, love, and joy in God's Word. He will show you the way.

I often seek out passages of scripture that speak to my current circumstance. It is amazing how God gives me a word for that moment.

Rest assured, you will not have to search through the Bible all day. Simply spend quiet time listening for His voice. It does not happen overnight, though. It's a learning process…and well worth the lesson.

LEARNING PROCESS

My Exodus: My Journey to Freedom

When my children's friends came to our home, I would cook and then retreat to my room, where I would sometimes stay for days at a time. I did not want to embarrass them, so I stayed out of sight. I felt bad about not being able to connect with them because they didn't want to talk to me.

While I was hiding away in my room, my children would be in the living room playing their games. Each had their own gaming system—something I felt would help ease the pain. They played their games, listened to their iPods, and texted on their cell phones. Sometimes, they would go outside into the yard to play basketball or jump on the trampoline. I would watch from my bedroom window and see how happy the three of them were before sneaking out to grab something to drink from the refrigerator then hurrying back to the confines of my room.

All the while, I sunk deeper and deeper into depression.

I continued studying my Bible during those times, allowing God's Word to get into my spirit. I would turn up the praise and worship music as loud as it could go.

Even now, my son tells me, "I remember being woken up in the morning for school with praise and worship."

We used to have Bible drills and devotions in the morning as a family. We needed as much of God's Spirit as we could get in our home.

TRIBULATIONS

I knew my husband was cheating on me. He would go away on long fishing trips or say he was at the barbershop and that the line was long—but come home without a haircut!

I could smell her on him.

The voices, of course, had their way with me. I often prayed hard, all while the spirit of manipulation led me down a crash course.

The lies… So many lies. The voices would often uncover his misdeeds. Many things weren't revealed until much later after he was out of my life.

Being that I wasn't fully delivered, my dreams tormented me while I slept. When he was around, all I wanted to do was sleep. That was a place of comfort.

He played with my mind, too. He would say he told me something or vice-versa, and I could not remember whether or not it happened. Again, I lost touch with reality. For example, I knew there were events taking place, but he somehow convinced me they weren't.

One thing my husband knew was that I could "feel" things. A memorable experience was when he and I were resting before work (we both worked the night shift at the time). Suddenly, I heard a voice call out, "CJ IS HURT!" The voice was clear as day. I immediately stirred out of my sleep, confused. My children were with their dad for the weekend. Later that evening, I received a call. CJ was hurt.

The next morning, my ex-husband brought my son home. I drove CJ to the hospital and learned his wrist was broken. He was waiting for me to overreact as I typically did when it came to my children, but I didn't. God humbled me. Once again, CJ had to return to an Orthopedic Specialist. We thought he would have to have surgery, but God intervened on our behalf.

I believe God showed us favor because we did not entertain Satan. What the enemy meant for evil, God turned it around for our good.

Things began to spiral more out of control in my life.

- On the job, the rumors were rampant about my husband cheating on me.
- My mother and sister were both in and out of the hospital.
    - One would go in for Congestive Heart Failure, and then the other would go in for the same condition.
- Another sister was in and out of the hospital suffering from health issues.
- I was suffering from mental issues.

Each time someone fell ill in my family, whatever the illness was would plant a seed in my mind. The voices told me I was the reason they were sick, to include blaming me for my mother's illnesses. She always worried about me, wondering when I was going to lose control again. I practically lived at the church, trying to keep depression and anxiety from overtaking me.

I feared losing my mother or sister. They were the ones holding me together. I needed them. That did not stop me from distancing myself, though. I felt they did not want me around. I just knew they were trying to leave me.

Things were so bad between my husband and me that I sent my children to live with my mother. I slept in the bedroom, and he spent most nights on the sofa. That was the best arrangement for us anyway because I didn't want him anywhere near me. Each time he went out, I knew he was with "her." The voices told me. When I asked him about it, he would always lie.

There was a time when my daughter had a band trip. At the time, we had two trucks: one old, one new. The old truck needed some work, but I was willing to drive it to San Antonio just to be with my daughter. The voices made it their business to tell me my husband didn't care about me, for he always took the best of everything and left my children and me with the worst.

Well, GOD worked it all out!

A compassionate school board member had taken notice of my support with many fundraisers. Every game my daughter went to, I was there. I joined Band Booster and was a faithful member, doing whatever needed to be done. When I told her I was going to drive that broken truck to San Antonio on sheer faith, believing for a miracle after praying with my prayer partner, the next thing I knew, we were all riding in two nice shuttle buses. No one had to drive their own vehicle! Thank You, Lord!!!

While away, the voices told me my husband was with his girlfriend. By that time, I had gotten so used to covering my pain. I totally focused on Tiara and Zaconey, ensuring they enjoyed the trip. CJ wasn't with us because he attended a different school. The agreement was that my husband would check on CJ while we were gone.

The voices told me to call his job. It must be noted that before we left, he would call me at 1:00 a.m. without fail, but since we were away, he did not call once. He didn't even call to see if we arrived safely. I called my prayer partner and asked her to pray with me before making the call to his job. Once done, I then placed a three-way call with her on the other line. I knew in my heart he wasn't going to be there. When security answered the phone, they told me he was off for a week on vacation.

The anger, hurt, anxiety, headache, and manic state I thought I would be in did not occur while I was away. I had peace. I went about each day as if nothing happened. I called to check on CJ, my mother, and the rest of the family. No one could tell something was wrong.

After placing second in the band competition, we returned home. My husband had yet to make it back, as he thought we were coming back the next day as scheduled. We made it home around 11:00 a.m., and the children went to school. He returned around 2:00 p.m. When I asked him if he missed us, I could tell he was a nervous wreck. He told me he had just come back from fishing. I clearly remember it was raining that day.

"Oh. You were fishing in the rain?" I asked.

He was quick with his lie. "It wasn't raining where I was at."

As I made my way to my room, I told him what I already knew. "You haven't been to work all week. You've been on vacation."

My sister's arrival was right on time because the argument between my husband and I was getting heated. To settle it once and for all, I said to him, "Let's just call your job!"

He, of course, declined.

I dropped the subject and went into my room. I knew then our season was drawing to an end, although we stayed together a little while longer.

We had a death in the family out of town and prepared to travel to South Carolina for the service. One of my favorite cousins passed away. He wasn't much older than I. My husband accompanied us on the trip. We showed up like we were a happy family. I hate pretending. I already had problems differentiating reality from imaginary. We stayed at my cousin's house with some other family members. I did the usual: stayed to myself.

At the service for my cousin, I took it badly. I could not believe my cousin was gone forever. My husband was there to comfort me. I sank into a severe depression, yet I continued to press my way through each day.

A few months later, my godson asked to come stay with us during the summer. My husband said no at first. After seeing how bad his denial hurt me, he agreed to let my godson come and stay. I was so happy to have him there with me again! The voices, depression, and anxiety completely left for about two weeks, and then all hell broke loose.

My godson got into some trouble and had to leave for a while. That August, my great-aunt passed away. I was still grieving the loss of my cousin. It was too much!

My husband promised he would take me to my aunt's funeral and help me deal with the issues going on in my life. Instead, he added more fuel to the fire. He stated there was a riot at work and that since he was on the S.W.A.T. team, he had to go in. He never called me back. I was concerned something happened to him but went to the funeral without him. When I left the service, I called him at work. Again, I learned he lied, telling his job he needed some time off due to a death in the family.

I remember the date very well: August 18, 2012. Anxiety's grip grabbed hold and wouldn't let go.

On August 22nd, I'd had enough and changed the locks on the door, effectively locking him out of the house. He countered by cutting the phone lines, turning off the lights, and removing the vehicles' relays. He then called me all sorts of names and cursed me out from top to bottom.

I refused to allow him to push me over the edge to wanting to hurt myself. I knew too much of God's Word and chose to dive in even deeper to nourish my spirit.

I studied Isaiah 54 in its entirety. Then, I was led to Amos 3:3 — we were no longer equally yoked. I reviewed Matthew 19:1-10, trying to get a revelation about marriage and divorce. Next, I went to 1 Corinthians 7:1-5, Ephesians 5:22-33, and 1 Peter 3:1-7. I studied to show myself approved to God.

I had to fight off what I felt was a losing battle against the disease's wickedness known as mental illness. I did everything possible to line up with the Word of God.

My husband had already moved in with his girlfriend, so THAT weight had been lifted. BUT the voices in my head told me, "Your children are getting older. They see how he treats you. It's now or never." From that point forward, I started having hallucinations of someone getting hurt. It seemed so real. Still, I praised God for it all. That man was finally out of our lives!

MOURNING

In 2013, I sank into a depression that was so severe and unlike any other time before. That time, it felt 100 times worse. Even with God's Word, I was at a point of no return.

In June, my prayer partner's father was killed the same day my grandmother and dog died.

My godson was killed on September 10th. Early that morning, my sister called me to tell me he had been killed at a McDonald's restaurant in Houston.

I was crushed. All at once, the voices, headaches, mania, anxiety, depression, anger, and bitterness struck. I didn't eat or sleep. I didn't read my Bible. I laid in the bed and stared at the ceiling in the dark, just as I usually did. As expected, the bed began to shake, and the demons were pulling me through. I really didn't care. I was hurting. The voices and dark spirits worked collectively to overtake my body. My bed was wet from countless tears, sweat, and urine, but I didn't move. I remained in the waste of grief, not wanting to go on with life.

When things happened in my life, I liked the comfort of having my room dark. I actually have black curtains in my bedroom. I loved lying in the dark as I thought about things. I found peace in doing so. I often drifted away into my fake world. It would be just me there, and I wouldn't have a care in the world.

Other days, my head would hurt so bad, I would have to close my eyes and force myself not to think terrible thoughts. I saw horrifying things that left me terrified for days or months, thinking something bad was going to happen.

My Exodus: My Journey to Freedom

"For God has not given us a spirit of fear, but of power and of love and a sound mind"
(2 Timothy 1:7, NKJV).

When my Uncle Boa passed away, my mother could not attend the funeral because she had breast cancer and was on dialysis. Those of us who could traveled back to South Carolina for his service.

At the time, I was dealing with so much. I was under attack again and felt as if the illness was overtaking me. Although I continued going to Texas MHMR, it seemed I was getting worse by the minute. I couldn't think clearly. I couldn't even focus on my oldest son's accomplishment of graduating from high school because my attention was placed on the bad things all around me.

I faithfully served God, unaware that my children knew about sex. Thankfully, the Holy Spirit prepared me for the events that were to come.

As I talked to my sister and two younger children, I told them my oldest son's girlfriend was pregnant. They laughed at me. They know I hear voices, so I suppose they thought it was just one of them speaking out. Still, I heard the message clear as day: She's pregnant. When I asked her, of course, she said she wasn't.

February 16th, I received a phone call from her telling me she's pregnant. As stated, I was already prepared for that news.

I must say here that I am so proud of my son. He was a teen parent who finished school and is a good father to his daughter. While in school, he stepped up and got a job to help support his child.

In 2012, while my marriage was falling apart, God sent me one of the biggest blessings I have in life. On May 4th of that year, God gave me my granddaughter, E'Mari Nicole Jackson. I love her so much. Through all the pain I was enduring, God gave me beauty for my ashes. Mari was my blessing in the middle of a raging storm. When my husband left, I was relieved. No tears of sadness fell from my eyes. I wanted him to be happy and knew I could no longer fill that space in his life. The infatuation and love we once shared were completely gone.

Our divorce proceedings began. We went to court several times in the process. I recall one time, I had my petition typed up and laid out very well. It seems I made a mistake, though, when I requested spousal maintenance as I presented my case. The judge saw me as an angry, bitter woman trying to cash in on my soon-to-be-ex's money. At the time, I was on disability and didn't work. The judge denied my request.

On June 16, 2014, my second divorce was finalized. I pretty much let him have whatever he wanted. I didn't even ask for any of his retirement or anything else. I just wanted the relationship to be officially over.

God truly blessed me, even though I felt the court and my ex-husband had wronged me. My relationship with God grew closer and more intimate through that experience.

Normally, I would have been so distraught, I would jump into my bed and hide under the covers. Were it not for God, I probably would have ended my life because I was humiliated by the judge. He did not know my story and didn't want to hear it, either. Suffering from mental illness and already thinking the world is out to get me could have made room for the judge to add fuel to the growing fire in my soul, but glory to God, it didn't.

NEW BEGINNINGS

God's presence entered my life. He spoke to me softly and gently, saying, "Liza, I will restore unto you the years the locusts and cankerworm did eat" (referencing Joel 2:25). He went on to say, "I will restore everything you have lost and more. Just trust me."

"Trust in the Lord with all your heart. And lean not on your own understanding; in all your ways acknowledge Him, and He shall direct your paths. Do not be wise in your own eyes; fear the Lord and depart from evil"
(Proverbs 3:5-7, NKJV).

My sister called me one day and said, "Let's go back to school."

Both of us had been out of school for over 25 years. We had to retrieve our old school records and make sure our paperwork was complete. Then, we had to wait to be accepted. Believe me when I say it wasn't easy, but God did it!

I returned to school in the Spring of 2015. It felt strange sitting in a classroom with people my children's age and younger. When the voices spoke, I quoted God's Word to them: "You must submit to the will of God!"

"I will instruct you and teach you in the way you should go; I will guide you with My eye"
(Psalm 32:8, KJV).

I knew the only way I could make it was with God's direction and Him leading my path while speaking to me.

Admittedly, I have many challenges. God, however, found me worthy to open so many doors and place people on my path.

My new educational venture was to work toward getting a degree in Criminal Justice. Many people advised against it, saying that I would not be able to work in the profession with me having a criminal record.

The voices began tormenting me again. "You're useless. Why even bother?" they taunted.

I used God's Word to combat that negativity.

"I know your works and what you are doing. See! I have set before you a door wide open which no one is able to shut; I know that you have but little power, and yet have kept My Word and guarded My message and have not renounced or denied My Name"
(Revelation 3:8, AMP).

I went to job fairs, and each employer told me the same thing: Having an assault on my record prevented me from working for their department. There was one nice woman I spoke with named Ms. Kelley, who worked for the Bryan Police Department. She listened as I explained how I obtained the charges I had on my record and that they dated back to over 15 years ago.

"We go through cycles," she explained. "That should not keep you from working a career in law enforcement. Follow your dreams. There are desk jobs and other positions you could hold."

Ms. Kelley spoke life into me. I often see her on our local news, reporting on robberies and homicides. I asked God to bless her, just as she did me that day. She does now know the impact she made on my life. I can only hope I can impact someone else's like as she did mine.

Sometime later, after the job fairs, we were assigned to write a research paper or intern at a facility. My professor told me I had to do the report because I would not be able to participate in the internship program. She knew my criminal background and mental illness issues would follow me.

Many organizations came and gave presentations to the class. The one where my professor once worked piqued my interest the most, and I was interested in interning there. I knew not to dare ask because she already told me it wasn't an option.

Later, I put in for the intern position anyway. As the supervisor walked me around, he said, "It seems you're the only one interested. You should have no problem getting the position." Since I would be interning for a grade, it would help not only me but also them. Before completing the paperwork, I told him about my background. Not long after, I received notice from Human Resources that I did not get the position.

I was hurt but determined. I really didn't want to write a research paper. I wanted the hands-on experience. I wanted to make a difference in people's lives, even though I fight with a disease of the mind.

I put in for another position and received a call the next day stating my criminal record was, indeed, a problem. I was persistent, though, and was encouraged by one of Jesus' parables as told in Luke 18:2-8 (AMP):

"He said, in a certain city, there was a judge who neither reverenced and feared God nor respected or considered man. And there was a widow in that city who kept coming to him and saying, Protect and defend and give me justice against my adversary. And for a time he would not; but later he said to himself, Though I have neither reverence or fear for God nor respect or consideration for man, Yet because this widow continues to bother me, I will defend and protect and avenge her, lest she give me intolerable annoyance and wear me out by her continual coming or at the last she come and rail on me or assault me or strangle me. Then the Lord said, Listen to what the unjust judge says! And will not (our just) God defend and protect and avenge His elect (His chosen ones), who cry to Him day and night? Will He defer them, and delay help on their behalf? I tell you; He will defend and protect and avenge them speedily. However, when the Son of Man comes, will He find (persistence in) faith on the earth?"

At the facility where I wanted to intern, I ran across the location's organizer and told him my story. He was a God-fearing, noble man who told me he would introduce me to the superintendent and explain to him what I shared.

I prayed about my interview with the superintendent. I knew the chance meeting with the organizer had to be God's doing.

The day came when I presented myself to the superintendent. He was a nice man who treated me with dignity and respect. Guess what? I was approved for the internship! I loved my time there — and made an A on my final! Thank You, Lord!!! I believed God was setting up something for me.

Later, I needed to intern for another class. My professor directed me to put in for Phobes Home. I explained my background during the interview, and the woman said, "The position is yours. I just have to wait for the background check to come back." That afternoon, she called me back and stated my background kept me from getting the position.

I called my professor and told her, "It looks like my Spring internship fell through." Three days later, she called me back and told me the other lady who was going to do the internship where I previously mentored had canceled.

Look at God!

All I had to do was the formality of interviewing for the position. I scheduled an interview, but it was canceled. A woman I had grown fond of at the facility had a death in the family. I didn't allow the situation to discourage me, though. A short time later, she called me back and said I came highly recommended by staff members at that location — and that I did not even need to interview! The position was mine!

God, I bless Your Holy Name!

I loved everyone I came in contact with while at Brazos County Juvenile Services. Everyone there spoke life into me and genuinely cared about each other. They treated each other as family, not just coworkers.

On my last day there, the judge sat and talked to all of us interns, describing her job in detail. I often witnessed her duties — something she always did with compassion, no matter the case that was put before her. I remember times when tears fell from my eyes while in her courtroom. I often sat in the back and hoped no one would see. It was as if the court system cared more about the individuals than they did themselves. Their nonchalant attitudes surely pained their parents. After all, who wouldn't want their children to do better?

HARDSHIPS

My Exodus: My Journey to Freedom

While attending school for my degree, I worked very hard and made good grades. During that time, my cousin's five children moved in with me for nine months. My daughter and I loved those babies. We gave them all we had…and things we did not as well.

Their living with me put us in a horrible financial situation. Two of them wore diapers at the time. Only one was going to school, and I had to take two weeks off from my studies due to not having a babysitter. The first two weeks in my home, the babies needed me as much as I needed them. My daughter continued attending school and was a faithful worker in her church at the time, so I had the babies MOST of the time while trying to complete my assignments.

Child Protective Services (CPS) would not allow just anybody to keep the children. They had to have an intense background check performed. Besides, no one wanted to care for five babies at one time. My mother and sister already took care of my sister's baby while she went to work. Still, both of them helped Tiara and me out a lot with them.

Although I was missing many days from school, my professors understood and helped as much as possible. On crucial days when I had to be in class, they allowed me to bring the babies in with me.

Thank You, Lord! He opened another door for me! That is the favor of GOD, not man.

When the children had to go to CPS, there were times when we did not have enough gas to take them, but God always seemed to make a way. Often, my children would give me the funds needed to gas up my car and go. One day, my sister-in-Christ called me to the back at daycare and gave me $50.00. She was a full-time teacher but worked at the daycare during the summer months. The Lord knew I needed the money, but I told her we were okay and refused to take it.

"Liza, don't tell me how to spend my money," she said.

Her kindness brought tears to my eyes. I had to set my pride to the side because I didn't have gas, and the babies were running low on diapers. Not only did she help us, but our church family also assisted us here and there. The daycare they attended belonged to the church's pastor and his wife—yet another door opened by God Himself.

When my cousin called and said she needed help for a little while with her children, I immediately went into prayer and asked God for His favor. I knew I had to have enough faith to believe God would allow them to come to stay with me because, previously, I'd been turned down so many times due to my criminal background. I didn't realize at the time why God told me no.

Let me explain.

In 2010, my husband (at the time) and I tried to become foster parents, attending several classes on Saturdays. My husband made many sacrifices for me. He would get off work after putting in an eight-hour shift and then go to a parenting class so we could try to adopt a child. However, my background came back, preventing me from moving forward once again. Nonetheless, I thanked God and prayed someone else would bless the child we were trying to adopt. To this day, I still think about him and pray for God's covering over him.

So, there I was, living my new life as a single woman, enrolled in school, and without the benefit of the income my ex-husband (who worked for the prison system) had.

I searched God's Word and was led to Luke 5:17-19.

"Now it happened on a certain day, as He was teaching, that there were Pharisees and teachers of the law sitting by, who had come out of every town of Galilee, Judea, and Jerusalem. And the power of the Lord was present to heal them. Then behold, men brought on a bed a man who was paralyzed, whom they sought to bring in and lay before Him. And when they could not find how they might bring him in, because of the crowd, they went up on the housetop and let him down with his bed through the tiling into the midst before Jesus" (NKJV).

You may wonder how that passage of scripture fit my situation. Well, it was what the Lord gave to me! I needed to walk a faith walk. God was the friend who carried us every single day. He was the friend who opened the door for the babies to come. God showed me He is God!

Two weeks before the babies returned home, my water was turned off. I never had the water turned disconnected in my home before that time — ever. That time, I did not have the money to pay the bill. To compensate for the lack, I would store water in the trunk of my car inside an empty container I filled at my ex-brother-in-law's house or my mother's home, although I did not want her to know my water was off.

As well, my house payment was three months behind. A charity and my sons helped me get caught up.

It was a serious faith walk.

While the babies were with us, Tiara was offered a job at the daycare. I can't thank her enough for all the sacrifices she made for us, including when her car broke down while they lived with us. We had to make two trips to transport the children back and forth to daycare because all five required a car seat.

I fondly remember the days. The babies would fight amongst themselves every morning and then all day, every day. "Don't touch me," they used to say to each other.

I was blessed with an amazing support group. A husband and wife from Voice for Children loved the babies just about as much as we did. They were the ones who helped get my water turned back on after learning we had no water in the home. CPS was aware as well and would tell me to "hang in there."

I knew my time with the babies were coming to an end. I could not continue to support five babies, my daughter, and myself while continuing my studies. My family, children, and the church helped as much as possible, but my responsibility wasn't theirs. I'm also grateful to Mr. Bart and Mrs. Manuela for their support during that time.

While the babies were with me, CPS gave me two gift cards totaling $650.00 and diapers, wipes, and Pull-Ups here and there. As well, when my car was broken down, they asked an organization to fix my vehicle. As "payment," I had to like their Facebook page and write a Letter of Appreciation—both of which I was more than happy to do.

On November 17, 2017, the babies returned home. My heart was heavy. The night before their departure, all five of them laid in the bed with me, and I prayed over them. While they were with me, I taught them their prayers, which I had them say each night. I typically read the biblical stories of Jonah in the whale or the Parable of the Lost Sheep. That night, I did not read the stories. I simply told them how much I loved them and that if they ever get into trouble, cry out, "JESUS! JESUS! JESUS!" and God would answer.

I did not sleep at all that night. I chose to watch over and continue to pray for them…and me.

RELEASING

The day the babies returned home, I had to first go to court. I cried the entire way there. I prayed and asked God to please give me strength and not to let my emotions take over.

When I entered the courtroom, I told everyone who asked that I was fine—but I wasn't. I couldn't provide for the children. My water was still turned off. My daughter's car was broken down. I almost lost my house. I didn't even have enough gas in my car to get back home. I was a failure. What could be "fine" about that?

We were called before the judge, and when he began asking questions, I began to cry uncontrollably. I had failed the babies. Plus, the voices had returned. I was hurting. We managed to make it through the proceedings, with me crying the whole time. All I thought about was the babies leaving my care.

As I left the courthouse that day, a police officer placed money into my hands. I was so distraught, I didn't realize just how much he gave me. While driving home, my car's low-fuel light began to ding. I pulled into the closest gas station, looked at the money in my hand, and thanked God for the $60.00 the officer gave me. I asked God to bless that officer and everyone who was in the courtroom. God used that man! I knew going in that I did not know how I would get back home on the fumes my car was rolling with. I had no money. I only had a prayer— one that God answered.

Later that day, I picked up the oldest two from school and then the other three from the daycare. I told Tiara I wanted to be alone with them. I remember we ate chili cheese dogs, and me allowing them to drink all they wanted. We also had ice cream and watched the Disney movies, "Frozen" and "Cars." I wanted the last few moments of them spent with me to be memorable ones.

The night wore on, and the children's father had yet to come to pick them up. Around 7:30 p.m., I went to Friday night Bible Study. I knew God would give me relief from the pain I felt, and He did just that. He spoke softly and gently, reminding me I wasn't a failure and that He was taking me places. He showed me that no matter what came my way, He would always be with me. He reminded me of how I welcomed the babies into my home and loved them with an everlasting love. When they were sick, I held them in my arms and prayed.

As stated, I'm grateful for the good people God placed in my life. Mr. Bart and Mrs. Manuela called to give me words of encouragement along the way. Not only did they gain the children, but they also gained me as well.

In May 2018, I graduated from Blinn with an Associate's Degree in Criminal Justice. I then transferred to Sam Houston State University.

BLESSINGS AND MORE BLESSINGS

My first week at Sam Houston was truly hectic. I didn't know where to park. I didn't know where any of my classes were. I knew no one there. I received a parking ticket for parking in the wrong zone. All my classes were early in the day. I truly wanted to quit. "This isn't for me," I said to myself.

The next week, I told my professor I was thinking about quitting, explaining the previous weeks' events. She was so kind and applauded my courage to return to school after being out of the loop for so many years. I shared with her the many struggles I had in life, and she was the one who convinced me to hang in there.

"If you need anything, do not hesitate to ask," she offered.

She was a woman of her word. Whenever I didn't understand something, she took the time to break it down for me. Many of my classmates asked how I understood her deep accent (she was from China). I had no problem understanding her because, after all, I'd been listening to different voices all my life. I loved both her and her accent. Plus, she genuinely cared about her students and their success.

The time came in my life when the voices I spoke to were real and anointed. One woman I can't thank enough is Charity Walton. She spent many hours praying for my family and me. She prayed I would succeed and encouraged me not to give up. Every program I told her I was considering, she would say, "Let's go into prayer." Immediately, she would pray for me.

I also had Ms. Dorothy praying for my daughter's safe return. Thank God for those prayers because it was my daughter who prayed me through many stressful nights.

When God spoke to me again, He directed me to read Jeremiah 29:11:

"For I know the thoughts and plans that I have for you, says the Lord; thoughts and plans for welfare and peace and not for evil, to give you hope in your final outcome" (AMP).

God gave me precisely that: hope. He provided for me and used my earthly father to bless me. You see, my father served in the U.S. Army and received an Honorable Discharge, which enabled me to attend school because they paid for 150 credit hours through the Hazelwood Act. The backstory is rather remarkable.

I was in class one day, and some young ladies were discussing how thankful they were for the Hazelwood Act because it helped them pay for the cost of school, all because of their parents' service in the military. When I told them my father served as well, they gave me a number to call and that it wouldn't hurt to see if I qualified. I went on to explain I had been married twice, never received any benefits from my dad through his service, and that he was 100 percent service-disconnected and on disability. Nonetheless, I got an application, took it to my father, and he filled it out. When I took it back to the college, in less than a week, I was approved.

That was God's favor and the Luke 2:52 blessing! Glory be to God!!!

God blessed me to become a part of TRIO—a program for first-generation students whose parents never obtained a degree. One could also qualify if they had a learning disability or were a low-income student. Not only was I blessed to be a part of the TRIO family, but I also became a TRIO Ambassador!

I was an Ambassador for Jesus Christ and TRIO! Look at God! Hallelujah!!! Hallelujah!!! Hallelujah!!!

So, not only was I attending Sam Houston State University and excelling in my studies, but I was also on the Criminal Justice Dean List in the Spring of 2019! I give ALL praises to God!

I also received a Spirit Award in TRIO. The award was presented by another person who changed my life.

The week I wanted to quit, I talked to my advisor. As I sat in her office crying my heart out, she told me to hang in there and that she was there if I needed her.

During my senior year, all kinds of challenges piled one atop the other. Family members died. I had a car wreck. Illness. Birth of grandbabies. I had exceeded the allotment in Pell Grants, so I was told I had to come up with $2,046.00 at once.

I thank God because only He could make a way out of no way.

Ms. Franz worked with me, and, with God's grace, the bill was paid in full.

The challenges didn't stop there, though. I struggled in Zoology and Statistics—two of my most challenging classes. Plus, I had a sick family member to contend with at the same time. But God! He is always an on-time God! With His guidance, I mastered all my classes with A and B averages.

On March 16, 2020, I was accepted into the Criminal Justice Master's Program at Sam Houston State University. On May 8, 2020, I was scheduled to walk across the stage to receive my Bachelor's Degree in Criminal Justice, but because of the Coronavirus, I was unable to do so until July 2020.

I cannot thank God enough. I truly know something about God's grace!

JOY, YET PAIN

On November 19, 2019, I received my class ring. The same day some 15 years prior, I was reminded of when I tried to take my own life, but God blessed me with exceedingly, abundantly more than I could ask or think.

Thank You, Lord! I cannot do anything but praise our God Almighty!

When I received my college class ring, I thought about my high school ring and how it was stolen from me.

This is not the first book I have written. I authored a book in 2013 — one I worked on when I was going through some dark days in my life.

Rains from May 2016 floods broke my home's air conditioner. In June, my sister was hospitalized and, after her release, stayed with her in her home to help out. My sons were using my car to get back and forth to work.

In July 2016, my home was broken into.

I was at my sister's house when my son called and asked, "Mama, where are our televisions?"

"Quit playing!" I told him.

"No, mama. I'm not. Our televisions are gone."

"Quit playing with me, CJ! Who's going to take a 73-inch television?" Everyone who lived around us was like family. They knew my sister was sick and that I was away, helping her.

In fact, I asked my ex-brother-in-law to keep watch over my house while I was gone. I called the police.

Shonte rushed me home. We arrived before the police. When I walked through my door, sure enough, everything of value was gone:

- The $500.00 in the safe the insurance inspector had just given to me for my damaged air conditioning unit, refrigerator, and some other things that were damaged in the May storm.
- The groceries I just purchased.
- The televisions in every room.

That was on Friday, July 15th. In my haste to leave, because I had a long trip the next day, I left the class rings behind. I thought I had them with me because I had shown them to the authorities while they were at the house.

The following day, I returned home at around 4:00 p.m., intending to clean up from the break-in. Wouldn't you know, someone broke into my home again and took everything of value that was left, including my children's and my class rings, computer, underwear, pots, pans, and everything else imaginable. They didn't just take my "stuff," they took my sanity, too. Those incidents nearly pushed me over the edge.

I tried thinking about the Lord, but all I could feel was hurt and pain. How could those monsters do that to me? Why me?

The voices reappeared and told me I was unsafe. Those demons came into my home and stole those class rings…and my peace. It wasn't as much about the rings' loss as it was the sentimental value attached to them. Those were some tough times. My mother sacrificed a lot, and my ring could never be replaced. The insurance paid Herff Jones to replace my children's rings, but since mine was made over 25 years ago, they did not have the record on file.

"That's what you get," the voices said.

You see, earlier, I had asked my ex to help buy Tiara's ring. Because he didn't feel it was a necessity, he refused to contribute. So, after purchasing and receiving her ring, I gloated by putting on all of our rings (my children's and mine). God had blessed me to buy all three of my children's rings, all without their father's assistance. God always made a way.

The voices told me because I boasted to my ex, I was being punished.

Once settled back at home, the voices told me night after night that the thieves were still in my house. To this day, everywhere I go, I know that whoever broke into my home is "out to get me." They know what size underwear I wear. They know my likes and dislikes. They have tablets and a computer with all my personal information. The book I was writing and many photos I took were stored on the computer. They have a diary of my innermost thoughts that I kept on an iPad.

Daily, I wondered when the thieves would return. Will we be home, and they now know we are inside?

When I complained about the hurt of having my home broken into, a friend of mine reminded me of Philippians 2:14 when he said, "Liza, you say you know the Lord. You know you're supposed to do everything without complaining."

Sadly, I knew he was right. I should have praised and thanked God that no one was hurt. Still, the voices in my head said, "No, Liza! That is your house and your property! No one should be allowed to come in and invade your home. You can't do the same to them!" I didn't want to invade their home. What's theirs belongs to them. What's mine belongs to me. That very thought would haunt me for years to come.

As you might suspect, I suffered a mental breakdown. No one knew how badly I was hurting on the inside.

I walked into Somerville Church of God, where the First Lady told me, "I will be watching you. You are special." I did not feel special at the time. All I felt were the hurts and pains of life. However, that day, she spoke a blessing into my life. Each day, I walked around, believing I was, indeed, special.

Yes! Fearfully and wonderfully made, I am! Marvelous is God's works!

God truly blessed me with people who have changed my life. Today, He is still doing wonderful things for me. I ask God to help me remain faithful, trusting, leaning, and depending on Him. I know I can do nothing without Him.

I have laid in my own waste due to the voices in my head. There were countless times I was unable to attend functions outside the home. Now, as I look to God and His amazing grace and mercy, I know He is seeing me through every trial and every test. I now have a vision, just as it says in Proverbs 29:18:

> *"Where there is no vision, the people perish"*
> (KJV).

I will not perish. I have written down my vision. Although it will take time to fulfill, I'm going to wait for it.

"And the Lord answered me, and said,' Write the vision and make it plain upon tables, that he may run that readeth it. For the vision is yet for an appointed time, but at the end, it shall speak, and not lie though it tarry, wait for it; because it will surely come,
it will not tarry'"
(Habakkuk 2:2-3, KJV).

I now know that whatever comes is in God's hands. I am learning to move out of His way. I am also learning that whatever happens in life, I will be okay.

As my friend mentioned, when they stole all my belongings, I needed to continue giving God praise. It all belongs to God, anyway!

During my senior year at Sam Houston, my classes were so important to me. I stressed out everyone around me, wanting perfect grades. I had to ask God and them for forgiveness because I had lost my way. GOD is my way and way maker. He is my first love and my last. How can I not love someone who loves me through it all? I am a nobody who has been rejected more times than I can count, yet God changed me into somebody who will always know to put my trust in Him.

I lean not on my own understanding. If anyone questions if God is real, I will tell them MY GOD is a healer, provider, and way maker. I will testify of the times He brought me out of so many unfortunate situations—and how He is still bringing me out!

MY EXODUS

My Exodus: My Journey to Freedom

If you have ever felt inadequate, unloved, unappreciated, or disqualified, know that God can reverse those feelings. I have learned God does not look at our outward appearance, education, race, or gender. He looks at our hearts.

Always know God loves you.

"Before I formed you in the womb I knew you; before you were born, I set you apart; I appointed you as a prophet to the nations"
(Jeremiah 1:5, NIV).

God made each of us with a unique purpose. We must listen to Him to receive what He has just for us. He has plans to prosper us. We, however, must be willing to change our ways and not settle for less.

The first thing I had to do to effect change in my life was admit I had a problem I could not fix on my own.

"'Wash yourselves; make yourself clean; remove the evil of your deeds from before My eyes; cease to do evil. Learn to do good, seek justice, correct oppression; bring justice to the fatherless; please the widow's cause. Come now, let us reason together,' says the Lord. 'Though your sins are like scarlet, they shall be as white as snow; though they are red like crimson, they shall be like wool. If you are willing and obedient, you shall eat the good of the land'"
(Isaiah 1:16-19, ESV).

I now feel I am living in God's will. I refuse to settle for less than His best. I admit I suffer from mental illness, but I will overcome every trial and tribulation.

"'I have said these things to you, that in Me, you may have peace. In the world, you will have tribulation, but take heart; I have overcome the world'"
(John 16:33, ESV).

I know God to be true. Those around me know that as well. I am a witness for God through my life. I have been misunderstood by those around me. I struggled with mathematics. I have a criminal record and two failed marriages to my credit...

BUT GOD has delivered me from them ALL!

CLOSING PRAYER

Our Father, which art in Heaven, hallowed be Thou Name. Thou will be done. Humble Your servant to do Your divine will. No matter where life leads me, please continue to show me the way I should go. Never let me get ahead of myself, and never let me take any of Your glory.

I ask You to bless everyone who reads this and pray it makes a difference in their life.

I thank You, Lord. I bless Your Holy Name.

Amen.

My Exodus: My Journey to Freedom

www.ingramcontent.com/pod-product-compliance
Lightning Source LLC
Chambersburg PA
CBHW052110110526
44592CB00013B/1554